Reality Television & Representing Reality

Iona Rose Wheeler

Boom Graduates
An imprint of Boom Publications Ltd
272 Bath Street
Glasgow SCOTLAND
G2 4JR

Boom Academic Press and the logo are trademarks of Boom Publications Ltd.

Boom Publications Ltd is a more-than-profit company, dedicating over half our profits to university scholarships for underprivileged students worldwide. In order to offset our carbon footprint, we also pledge to plant a tree for each graduation book commissioned.

Reality Television & Representing Reality
was first published in Great Britain in 2022.

Typeset by Helen at Boom Graduates.
Printed and bound in the UK.
To find out more about our authors and books visit www.boomgraduates.com and sign up for our newsletters.

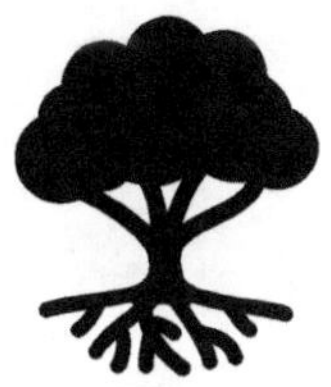

We plant a tree for every
Boom Academic Press book commissioned, and
thereafter plant a tree for every 10 books sold!

THG
(more : trees)

MEMBER

Watch our forest grow at
https://moretrees.eco/forest/BoomPublicationsLtd/

Iona Rose Wheeler

Reality Television & Representing Reality

Iona Rose Wheeler

Contents

Iona Rose Wheeler

Abstract

Reality television is a genre that represents real people and their real lives. But all representation is transformation, and television transforms reality into many different things. This dissertation looks at the cultural stimuli for reality-based media and how it is perceived, as well as exploring the idea of watching and being watched. Ideas of surveillance, identity, and reality itself are communicated through our screens, which affects the subjects and the viewers. There are also discussions surrounding who and what is represented, how and why this is done, and the consequences of doing so.

Iona Rose Wheeler

Introduction

Reality television claims to be a genre of entertainment that deals with actuality. Its prefix opposes itself to regular television, television with actors, scripts, and edits. It has real people with real stories. This gives us as viewers a sense of closeness, that we too could be on the screen, which is as alluring as it is frightening. If they are real people, they're just like us, and if they can get humiliated, shamed, and famous, we can too. But, despite its name, reality television is often scripted, and uses cinematic techniques, like framing, editing, directing, and voiceovers, to craft narratives. Knowing this, watching reality television gives viewers the same feeling as watching a film that preludes the audience with the phrase 'based on a true story'. It is reality transformed into something new. By representing real people through a screen, how do they change? And what impact does that have on those people and their viewers?

"All representation is transformation"[1]: there is no way to present reality in its wholeness, especially through a screen. I am interested in how a camera and crew deals with reality and its transformation. By focusing on reality television's relationships to women, panoptic surveillance policing, and marginalised groups, this book examines the reasons, methods, and consequences of representing the real. This is done by looking at reality television itself, other media centred in reality, and the history sounding them.

Chapter One:

Defining Reality Television

It is first necessary to define reality television and understand how it differs from documentary and other non-fictional moving image genres. There are a few existing definitions, because reality television is a newly named category. The 'first reality show' is contested. Do documentaries count? What about the news? In the case that all non-fictional television counts, there has been reality television for as long as there has been television. But the genre has morphed as the content, formats, and reception has solidified. Perhaps the difference is similar to a textbook and a biography, because both are concerned with the 'truth' but are produced and consumed in different ways. One distinction between reality television and documentaries, as they are widely understood, would be their subject matters. Reality television is concerned with the known, the mundane, and the domestic, whereas documentaries and docu-series seek to document the unknown, the extraordinary, and the outside. This binary is not all encompassing nor without its exceptions but separating the two categories could explain their respective reputations. The content of reality television and documentaries are the same, they are both concerned with the real. However, a quick search for academic articles about reality television brings up far less results than those about documentaries (a Google Scholar search of "allintitle: reality television" produces about 2,250 results whilst a search of "allintitle: documentary" produces about 78,800 results as of February 2022).

Gender studies and popular culture academic, Elizabeth Johnson, writes that "reality shows which focus on what might be considered feminine concerns – courtship, marriage, domesticity – would be considered the lowest of the low, eliciting even less critical attention", and that "the absence of scholarly work on what women watch no doubt can be blamed on the traditional assumption that what goes on in the privacy of the home ("women's space") is less important than what goes on outside it ("men's space").[2]

Even *Keeping up with the Kardashians*, the popular reality programme that follows the mega famous Kardashian matriarchy, is about the drama of their everyday. I put forward that subjects which are concerned with the mundane; making house, relationships, cooking, is consumed by women, because that has been the labour that women undertake. Why then would men find it worth researching? Connoting reality television, most of which is played during the day (daytime television), to women, is interesting, as it implies the existence of women in the house, where the television is, during the day. By contrast, prime time television is in the evening, the time where people are back from a typical nine-to-five day of work, is dedicated to fictional shows. Looking further into this gendered binary, we can draw similar parallels between the reputations of television and film. The television is the domestic to the worldly cinema.

Where films are traditionally viewed in public spaces, the men's space, the televised is brought into the home, the women's space. Kelefa Sanneh writes that "Reality television is the television of television,"[3] which encapsulates the view that this form of media is regarded as the lowest of the low.

As capitalism encroaches onto our every being, it is of interest to relate patriarchal pressures to capitalist ideals. "Although reality television is often mocked for its frivolity, Andrejevic argues that its success is symptomatic of an age in which labour and leisure are growing ever harder to separate."[4] Women are now expected to work double time, doing household, mothering, and emotional labour, as well as making a monetary income. With influencer culture allowing people to make money from sponsored posting on social media about products they use in their 'real' life, the lines between performed life and real life are near non-existent. This is what makes *The Real Housewives* franchise so fascinating. A pastiche of the fictional soap, *Desperate Housewives, The Real Housewives* began as a real life look into the lives of wealthy women. The cast members are filmed going about their everyday tasks, each episode usually leading up to them meeting with each other for dinner or drinks, then gossip, chaos, and drama ensues. The content is mostly about their interpersonal relationships, interspersed with trying an expensive new Botox or cryogenic beauty treatment. Layers of leisure, labour, spending, relationships, and mundanity amalgamate until we cannot unpick the truth from their performance. It is real, real relationships, real life hurdles, real(ish) people, formed into a flashy programme to be consumed. Just because their lives are compressed into a commercial programme that it should be viewed any lesser, but we can also critique the way that these women, these housewives, are packaged into consumables at the same time. There is space to enjoy these 'trashy' shows while analysing them through the lens of knowing that the platforming of absurdly rich and successful women is not necessarily a feminist 'win'.

The dramatisation, or any other representation, of the mundane could be a positive; it realises the lives of housewives as something worth paying attention to. But just because domesticity is platformed, its reception is not necessarily positive. The connection between women and the real is not new, as can be seen within the realism boom in Eighteenth Century novels. The novel "was often disparaged by literary critics, shunned as "low" art because of its thematic focus on domestic experience, as well as the fact that many eighteenth-century novels were written by women".[5] Women's entertainment being perceived as lesser was not born from reality television by any means.

Although the novels written in this era were fictional, the authors would allege that they were based in truth. They would write in first person, claim to be autobiographical or begin with a note letting the reader know that the following text had been found or transcribed from letters. This would give readers a feeling of intimacy, that they were being let in on a secret, not unlike reality programmes where viewers are let into the inside lives of someone else. Furthermore, readers of novels in the eighteenth century would be aware that the author was lying. "Most readers recognised that the letters/memoirs were fictional. Nevertheless, the frame was still necessitated; the fiction needed the appearance of reality".[6] We can compare this to the common reality television watcher today. With enough media literacy it is easy to see that a day, week, or month's worth of 'reality' must be heavily doctored to create an hour long episode of slick television. We know this, but it might not even matter.

We want entertainment! Perhaps the precursor of 'reality' does not change the television watching experience.

These differences between documenting and representing the real in terms of gender affect those who watch these shows as well as their creators. With reality television, we either want to see real people, like ourselves, or something we don't know. Perhaps women like to see themselves on screen because throughout history they have been erased from narratives. Part of the appeal of reality television is the allure that we too could be on the screen, if they are real people, they're just like us. It's attractive, to be invited into someone's home, and see their real life, with no expectation to show your own. The television is a symbolic one-way window, brought into the home.

Reality television in its literal state is television about reality. The specifics are socially and culturally enforced, but to discuss reality through a screen, a documentary shown on television, the morning news, and all other non-fictional television is reality television. I then ask you as a reader to understand the documentaries I discuss in the same vein as the programmes that are classified as reality television. Both are representations of reality in an audio and visual media. "All representation is transformation".[7] It is reality's transformation that I am interested in examining.

Chapter Two:

Surveillance

Moving from cinema to television, visual storytelling moved from public spaces into the private home. This mirrored the government's home intrusion with advances in technology. Bradley D. Clissold writes about the reality programme *Candid Camera*, the first reality programme of its kind, as a force of government and draws parallels between reality television and the public's fear of surveillance. One of the show's initial presenters and creator's, Allen Funt, was well versed in monitoring technology. His studies in Cornell used two-way mirrors and during his stint in the army he used microphones to record messages and conversations to create radio programmes. He learnt that the subjects of his recordings were more relaxed and talkative when he disabled the red 'recording' light of the microphone. This concealment of recording equipment was formative in the 'hidden camera' genre of reality media.

> The show began as Candid Microphone in 1948, just as classical Hollywood cinema entered its demise, at the beginning of television's household dominance and in response to Cold War fears of national security.[8]

Candid Camera used cameras to film people unknowingly in scenarios set up to create comedic scenarios, like a grandfather to *Impractical Jokers* and *Prank Patrol.* The subjects filmed were all given releases to sign after being filmed to consent to the sharing of their images. By letting them in on the 'joke' after it was played, there is some easing of consciousness, but then again, the joke was still played in the first place. The crew do not direct the subjects and their reactions are completely unscripted. But, by creating the settings, they guide the people within them, to get an entertaining outcome. This could by compared to posing questions in an interview. The interviewee is free to say what they will, while the interviewer may funnel this with their questions. The 'candid' nature of the show stays intact, but it is still artificial. Therefore, it is real, but the reality is crafted.

By filming people without their prior consent and showing it to the public and calling it entertainment, surveillance becomes something tangible and relatable. "The possibilities are limitless: the prospect is horrifying. Wait till they get the Candid Television Camera. You won't be safe in your own bathtub".[9] Rather than hearing whispers of the red menace invading the home, people were inviting it into their houses for entertainment. *Candid Microphone* was reformed as *Candid Camera* in 1949, the same year as George Orwell's novel *Nineteen Eighty-Four* was released. *Nineteen Eighty-Four* has become emblematic in discussing surveillance states and reality television, most notably in *Big Brother*.

Within the setting of *Nineteen Eighty-Four*, *Big Brother* is the omnipotent and omnipresent ruler, and seen in posters with the slogan, "BIG BROTHER IS WATCHING YOU".[10] This book was written to be a satire of communism but describes a dictatorship. The Godlike Big Brother is an exaggeration, or fictionalisation, of the totalitarian state of the USSR at the end of the Second World War. In the year 1999, Dutch television channel 'Veronica' aired a new show *Big Brother*, a social experiment televised. The concept was simple, put strangers in a house with no communication with the outside world and make them vote each other out until there's a victor. With over 500 seasons of the show airing around the world since then, *Big Brother* (the programme) is perhaps more culturally relevant today. There's a cyclical motion of life imitating art imitating life and on and on, when we look at the idea of *Big Brother.*

The University of Dundee, like many schools, has two anonymous confessional Facebook pages, *Dunfess* and *Dundate.* They are filled with short statements, the latter with lonely hearts-esque confessions about people on campus or in the general Dundee area. They range in anonymity, from a hair colour in the library, to initials, to a name, course, and location. This page has created a personal panopticon.

> As a work of architecture, the panopticon allows a watchman to observe occupants without the occupants knowing whether or not they are being watched.[11]

This idea of potential surveillance is prevalent within reality television and society in general with the existence of CCTV (Closed Circuit Television) and the Internet. We know that people we pass on the street will rarely look at us or even give us a second thought and yet, they could, and they could write about it on *Dundate*. These Facebook pages, in combination with the weight of the male gaze, leads to ruminating on what to wear or how to act whilst in public, because what if someone writes about it? Do *Love Island* or *Big Brother* contestants have this panopticon prisoner thinking, perpetually aware that their movements and words are being monitored, filmed, and potentially televised. I wonder if they must thrust themselves into a fugue state to deal with it and to what extent it influences their actions. It is surely easier to pretend that the camera is not there, that this is the new normal. It was hardly surprising that in the latest season the *Love Island* producers offered eight therapy sessions for each contestant.

The press around this decision stocked it up to the "potential negativity" in the 'outside world' that they may face. The catalyst for this was no doubt the suicides of three *Love Island* celebrities; Sophie Gradon and Mike Thalassitis, who were previous islanders, and the original host of the show, Caroline Flack.

Would the offered therapy focus on preparation for the inertia of fame in the outside world rather than the effects of their time in the villa? Also note that the therapy is not mandated. By it being only offered rather than mandatory, contestants may refuse that they 'need' the therapy because they are currently fine, instead of putting together a safety plan. This could affect the men more, as the internal stigma around asking for help as a man may prevent them from receiving it. *Big Brother* includes psychologists both onscreen, for special episodes, and offscreen. Sarah Angel was a resident psychologist on *Big Brother Australia*, and she said in a 2012 interview that competing on *Big Brother* is "something they're not prepared for. Not only do they not know what's been going on while they've been in the house, but they have to then deal with the quick aftermath of that (fame)".[12] Whilst the inclusion of psychology is admirable, one of the main benefits of therapy is having a confidential space, which is moot if it is televised. This could result in a public distrust of therapy if one's favourite 'reality' show shows no privacy in therapy sessions. Whose responsibility is it for participants to be emotionally safe? The individual who signs up, the producers, the public, the media?

We like watching people fall in love, but we like watching them fall out of it even more. There are scenes in *Love Island* where a couple has an argument, or an islander bursts into tears, and it is so awfully human. It's schadenfreude and voyeuristic, whilst underwritten with an overwhelming feeling that we should not be watching this. But you do, and it gets harder to look away as these real people become your favourite characters. At least for actors, they can physically remove themselves from their characters, and fans can love or hate what they see on screen without it being personal. But for reality stars, viewers feelings are direct, which can be psychologically damaging.

Are there examples of positive results from one thinking they are being watched? Indeed, in law enforcement the existence of CCTV and even the presence of 'Smile you're on camera' posters are crime deterrents. Within reality television a prime example of a positive panopticon is the reality programme *What would you do?* This hidden camera show poses actors in public spaces acting out conflicts, and films the responses from onlookers. They are then greeted by the host John Quiñones, told that they were being filmed, and asked about why they did or did not step in.

> The show has been going on for so long and it's so completely popular that in the latter seasons, people start intervening [be]cause they think that John Quiñones_is watching, which is basically like the idea of morality being created by god, except god is former ABC news host John Quiñones.[13]

A panopticon is form of crime prevention and in this case promotes people to intervene when they see someone acting unlawfully or in prejudice. Instead of enforcing the panopticon prisoners to not do something, *What Would You Do?* promotes action in aiding a stranger. The situations simulated are never foreign or artificial enough to illicit embarrassment like a prank, but, more often than not, show good human responses. Maybe an omni-everything first testament god is the original multi camera reality show inspiration.

Being watched is a cornerstone of religion and policing, the removal of an actual god or CCTV camera doesn't matter, we learn to police ourselves as we feel their ghosts. With no prestige of previous seasons, contestants take a bigger risk by participating. For recent and future contestants, becoming a reality star is a huge career move. Angel says of *Big Brother*,

> Some people are looking at it as an opportunity to have ongoing fame I guess, as a stepping-stone to potential jobs. Other people are just interested in it as a life experience and you get people motivated by the competition, playing

the game and getting the prize at the end.[14]

This puts into question the motivations of contestants and how they act within the programme. If there is money at stake, which there almost always is, people may change their actions to get further along in the competition. This sounds ill-natured but someone altering their personality to gain the public's affection is not much different than the actions of a salesperson. Reality television competition competitors have to sell themselves; they must create a celebrity out of themselves in order to survive.

Within the realm of dating programmes like *Love Island* or *The Bachelor*, getting to the final means finding 'love', and throughout each season, drama arises from questioning whether contestants are in it for the money or true love. Because of these shows' reputations and the ability to watch previous seasons, it becomes easier to 'play the game', and act untruthfully. Representing reality through television differs not only through the producers, editors, and others behind the camera, but also within the people being filmed. Knowing that you are being filmed will affect your actions, and making actions into performances is almost inevitable. This is expedited when people have previous notions of being perceived, like women having the pressure of the male gaze or people of colour having to code switch in order to feel safe.

There is power in filming. The person behind the camera has power over the person in front of it as they decide what reality will be filmed and how the subject is seen. There is abuse of power only where there is power. So surely without the tool of power, in this case the camera, there is no power to abuse. But a camera is not the only tool of power, there are much larger tools at play. Patriarchal, racist, colonialist, and capitalist powers are bigger than all of us, and taking away the camera often allows these powers to be unseen. For example, a white policeman harming a black civilian has the powers of whiteness, potentially gender and ability, and being a police officer in and of itself. If an onlooker were to film this abuse of power, this may give the onlooker some power, but it may not outweigh the police officer. It may deter the police officer from continuing but it may also make the onlooker a bystander. Similarly, the presence of

CCTV may alleviate some crime and will certainly help identify a criminal, but it will not eradicate crime or the circumstances that lead people to commit crimes. Does the camera's footage ease the pain of the victim, or does it just expose this pain to every viewer? Yes, footage of crimes can, in some cases, lead to the punishment of perpetrator, but that does not undo the action, let alone remove or change the powers that allow the abuse. Rehabilitation of the perpetrator or healing for the victim is not fulfilled by filming the crime, only punishment. A camera is a tool of power, but it is not the only in the shed. "Therefore it is useful to think of documentaries as exercises of power and examine the political and social consequences of this power".[15]

Within reality television, there exists programmes that capitalise on the drama of the criminal justice system, including genres like true crime, cop shows and court-based reality programmes. Crime based reality television is told from the perspective of the law enforcement, and uses both hidden camera footage, from CCTV and dashcams, and visible camera footage, such as talking heads, interviews, and re-enactments. Because these programmes rarely come from the viewpoint of the perpetrators or victims, and are under the pretence of 'reality', only one side of the story is told. This may fall under the term copaganda (portmanteau of cop propaganda). The use of hidden and visible cameras expedites the all-seeing nature of the government and instils the fear that not only will your crimes be seen, but they could also be televised.

Chapter Three:

Industry Conventions

To understand why reality television is the way it is, we must look at its production and the industry it exists within. How much responsibility does a company have to tell the honest truth? And what lengths must they go to get it? Marcel Ophüls wrote that "If being a gentleman is a documentary filmmaker's top priority, he'd better get into some other line of work"[16] and Stella Bruzzi calls documentaries "a negotiation between filmmaker and reality"[17]. It is suggested that for a filmmaker to take someone else's story and dilute it is ethically unsound, but what about the other workers within the reality television industry?

There is a refusal to call writers 'writers' within the reality genre. An edit is made to the role to create a sense of realness. Naming them 'story editors' allows for an illusion of sporadicity, that scenes are not created before they happen, but lightly edited afterwards. Although the cast on reality programmes like *The Real Housewives* are not actors by trade, they still do act out lines or scenes. Because a camera crew cannot follow the cast around twenty-four/seven, they may get the cast to re-enact conversations or scenarios.

One couple that went on the show *Couples Come Dine with Me* had been married, then divorced, then married again. During the pre-production process, they were told that they had to frame their divorce papers and put them on the wall. This was to spark a conversation in the segment where the guests snoop around their host's house. It was a clever set up by the producers, or writers. They weren't technically writing a script, but simply placing disclosed information on the wall, they could predict conversation and hopefully conflict. They were not writing fiction, but displaying an otherwise hidden truth to exacerbate it. Reality television is connoted with drama, but it is just condensing weeks or months of reality into a 'best of' montage. And it makes our real time lives seem dull in comparison, we only get drama once in a while! It's the "creative treatment of actuality".[18] It's editing real time into heightened hours of drama. The storylines are not created but shaped into something entertaining, something that can be watched and consumed.

> For a long time they (producers and networks) tried to keep the facade up that there was no writing in reality, that this was truly just putting a camera out there and recording and drama just happens.[19]

The elimination of 'writers' in the traditional sense is also the cause for the noughties boom of reality television unions. Television writers are usually a part of a writers' union to ensure fair pay, medical care, and general fair treatment. To date, the longest Writers Guild of America strike was in the eighties, mainly due to the lack of royalties paid to writers in the new market of VHS (Video Home System). Similarly, the 2007 WGA strike was influenced by the technological and capitalist introduction of DVDs (Digital Video Disk). DVDs were much cheaper to produce than VHS, so profit margins were much larger for film and television studios, but royalties remained at the same price.

Television companies didn't want to pay writers their dues, so they created shows that didn't require them. This meant that the renamed writers were hired under a different role, and not a part of the writers' union that guarantees their livelihoods. Making and saving money is always going to motivate artistic and cultural trends. "Reality works because it is relatively cheap to make".[20] The noughties golden era of reality television is linked to the underpayment of writers and following exploitation of younger workers in television, as well as the 2009 recession inspiring programmes like *The Real Housewives*. When a cultural phenomenon is grounded in underpayment and loopholes around free labour (no writers or actors) for monetary gain, it's no wonder that the genre is regarded as cheap and that every party involved is exploited in one way or another.

Chapter Four:

Representing Marginalised Groups

We have already established that "all representation is transformation",[21] but how does this affect groups that are already underrepresented? The 're' in 'representation' implies a filter in which the information we are presented with has gone through. For example, we get a show like *Ru Paul's Drag Race*, a reality competition that merges the likes of *America's Next Top Model, Pop Idol* and *The Real Housewives*, that thrives on its representations of queer performers. The first few seasons would only showcase gay cisgender men performing as women. When a contestant would incorporate masculinity into their look or come out as a transgender woman, the judges would criticise or eliminate them. In more recent seasons, contestants of all genders and sexualities have been introduced. However, with a plethora of reiterations and a solid formula that can be churned out, it represents, but also melds the uniqueness of drag performers and queer people into a consumable. It homogenises a community so large that one can hardly call it a community.

When participants are more often scouted than cast on their own volition, the idea that these are regular people feels less and less believable. Showing a group of very beautiful, able-bodied, thin people and telling the audience that these represent 'real' people is like telling them that if they don't look like that, there is something wrong. The contestants on *Love Island* and other reality dating programmes having a uniform look creates a standard that may imply that if someone is not as good looking as them, they are not worthy of love. Representing a person on television affects that person as well as the similar or unsimilar people that watch them.

The difference between diverse casting and representative casting is subtle but stark. Prior to the UK 2021 Summer series of *Love Island*, the producers boasted their "most diverse cast ever".[22] However, this resulted in the same amount of people of colour versus white people, the same slender body types and conventional beauty, but with one physically disabled islander. Diversity as a concept only works if you view able bodied, cis, straight, and white bodies as the norm and everyone else as diverting from the norm. Calls for 'more diverse casting' is accepting that whiteness is the norm, and everything else is other. It is also not representative casting as it does not accurately represent the population. Although more diversity and good representation would be a step forward within reality television, these things do not actively dismantle power structures or progress societies treatment of marginalised groups. This may be asking too much from an industry built on cheap entertainment, but is important to note nonetheless.

If we look at reality television in the same vein as documentaries, an early example of crafted narratives of a marginalised group can be found in the very first documentary. The first of fifteen documentaries directed by Robert J. Flaherty, *Nanook of the North* portrays the Indigenous people of Inukjiak. *Nanook of the North*'s tagline,

"A story of life and love in the actual Arctic",[23] contradicts itself and reveals how fickle the film is. Using the word 'actual' implies the film's verity, whilst 'story' tells us that it may be romanticised. The term 'documentary' was coined by a Scottish filmmaker, John Grierson, after seeing *Moana*, another film of Flaherty's. It was Grierson who described the documentary as being a "creative treatment of actuality",[24] and that actuality can be treated so much that it ends up as fiction.

The first few minutes of the film consist of title cards, written by Flaherty, describing his experience in filming, editing, losing, and refilming *Nanook of the North*. He calls the titular character Nanook (whose real name was Allakariallak but Flaherty changed it to Nanook, meaning polar bear, as it "seemed to suit the whites better"[25]) his 'character' and uses the colonialist term 'Eskimo' when referring to an Inuk. Already, Flaherty is telling his story of watching the Inuit, rather than their story itself.

In a later documentary, *Nanook Revisited*, filmmakers Claude Massot and Sebastian Regnier revisit Inukjiak almost seventy years after Flaherty. This 1990 documentary has the technological advantage of having non diegetic sound, allowing for the Inuit to speak for themselves rather than having their actions diluted by Flaherty's words. In one sequence, we see an Inukjiak local, Moses Nagawak, watching scenes from Nanook of the North and debunking their actuality. "Robert doctored this particular scene so that the image would fit the imagination. . . . This was staged. . . . It was a film for white people, Inuit customs alone were to be shown".[26] Hearing Nagawak correct so much of this 'documentary' puts into question the validity of the genre.

The film cuts between the original black and white footage of Allakariallak fighting with a rope going into a hole in the ice and new coloured footage recreating this, showing that the rope was fed through another hole and pulled by a few more people, imitating a fight with the seal they were hunting. This is an example of using the cinematic technique of framing to exclude information, creating a more pleasing narrative. The original scene portrayed the Inuit as struggling for food, which would have exacerbated stereotypes of indigenous peoples. The camera captures truth, and yes, Allakariallak was pulling a rope, that is truth, but it is not the whole truth. "Actuality is infinite and can never be wholly represented. Any representation is a selective view of the world".[27]

There is no such thing as reality through a screen, as the filmmaker has decided what to show and what to conceal, and a singular viewpoint can never be the truth. Even if we take out that the filmmaker is a person with unconscious (and often conscious) bias, a camera cannot film every physical viewpoint. There is a decision being made when framing a scene, and that affects the story and its implications.

But what do the filmmakers have to gain from lying? Well, there's money, fame, success, and the advantage of remaining the colonial power to name a few. Flaherty was aware of the attempted genocide of indigenous people in America, but refused to show them as equals, only allowing traditional tools to be filmed and exaggerating their struggles and 'primitiveness'. Since the genre of the documentary didn't exist as we now define it, there was no obligation to fit a pre-existing mould. There was no loyalty to 'truth'; Flaherty was just telling a story. And it was a popular story. Flaherty remains a pillar within film studies and *Nanook of the North* is considered to be the first documentary ever made. This film ensured Flaherty a filmmaking career, and his films continue to be classified as documentaries, whilst being rather removed from reality. Allakariallak died shortly after the filming and is widely known by another name. This film is probably a pebble in comparison to the planet that is colonisation but by being named a document of truth, it likely informed many people of the Inuit for the first time or shaped and solidified their already racist views. *Nanook Revisited* will also have many discrepancies, as it too is a retelling of the truth, but its aim is to correct and discuss the 'truth' of a previous documentary.

"All representation is transformation", not only in the distortion of reality through a camera, but in telling a story alone. The decision and dedication to film something, let alone create a whole series of television, is colossal enough to warrant meaning. The personal bias of a filmmaker will affect what they want to film and the decision to film one thing over another is a filtering of reality. Bias will always change what aspects of reality are chosen, filmed, edited, and distributed, therefore there is no truly neutral representation of reality in visual media, especially television which requires much funding and the backing of a broadcasting channel. So if there are no true representations of reality, why does good representation matter? Isn't a good story not enough? I argue not, especially when the story is told under a guise of 'reality'.

Representations of marginalised groups have been fundamental to popular media, but these groups are often represented by people out with the groups themselves. This means that people don't get to speak for or present themselves, and are in turn represented by their oppressors with their own motives. Misrepresenting the truth allows false narratives to remain and perpetuates bigoted and fascist views.

I do not rally for good representation in order to educate white, middle class, and Western viewers, but to create a mirror in which marginalised people can see themselves. By centring traditionally othered stories, telling them as truthfully as possible, and hiring people to tell them themselves, they become less like characters and more rounded, tangible, and real people.

48

Conclusion

Reality can never be fully presented through a screen, but efforts are still made by documentarists. There are many reasons as to why reality television may not aim to be as real as it could be. It is entertaining and captivating, exploiting the humanity of subjects and viewers alike. Watching those people makes us feel close to the people on our screens whilst forcing us consider how we too are perceived. It makes television corporations a lot of money due to its low production costs and has huge cultural value. Reality television is voyeurism at its core and there are many positions of power at play. By naming a carefully crafted piece of media 'real', we view it differently, and reality too becomes distorted. It's trashy, watchable, loveable and insane.

Endnotes

[1] Louise Spence and Vinicius Navarro, *Crafting Truth: Documentary Form and Meaning* (New Brunswick, N.J.: Rutgers University Press, 2011), p. 11.

[2] Elizabeth Johnston, "How Women Really Are: Disturbing Parallels between Reality Television and 18th Century Fiction", in *How Real Is Reality TV?: Essays on Representation and Truth* (North Carolina: McFarland, 2006), p. 116.

[3] Kelefa Sanneh, "The Reality Principle", *The New Yorker*, 2011.

[4] Mark Andrejevik, cited in Sanneh, "The Reality Principle"

[5] Johnston, "How Women Really Are", p. 116.

[6] *Ibid.*, p. 117.

[7] Spence, *Crafting Truth*, p. 11.

[8] Bradley D. Clissold, "Candid Camera And The Origins Of Reality TV", in *Understanding Reality Television* (London: Routledge, 2004), p. 33.

[9] Allen Funt and Philip Reed, *Candidly, Allen Funt: A Million Smiles Later* (New York: Barricade Books, 1994), p. 30.

[10] George Orwell, *Nineteen Eighty-Four* (New York: Secker & Warburg, 1949), p. 1.

[11] Thomas McMullan, "What Does The Panopticon Mean In The Age Of Digital Surveillance?", *The Guardian*, 2015.

[12] Sarah Angel, cited in Andrew Fenton, "The Psychologist Behind Big Brother", *News.Com.Au*, 2012 <https://www.news.com.au/entertainment/tv/psychologistbehind-big-brother/news-story/e193d00b9cc9a23be9917232d1a2e20c> [Accessed 6 February 2022].

[13] Pete Davis, "The John Quinoñes Panopticon", *Current Affairs*, 2022

<https://open.spotify.com/episode/1ibN7rfYEQVHX188HOCAwa ?si=XVeNEFiERviAx6eR zYc4-A> [Accessed 6 February 2022].

[14] Angel, cited in, Fenton, "The Psychologist Behind Big Brother".

[15] Spence, *Crafting Truth*, p. 86.

[16] Marcel Ophüls, "Closely Watched Trains", in *Claude Lanzmann's Shoah: Key Essays* (New York: Oxford University Press Inc., 2007), p. 83.

[17] Stella Bruzzi, *New Documentary: A Critical Introduction*, 2nd ed. (Abingdon: Routledge, 2006), p. 186.

[18] John Grierson, "The Documentary Producer", *Cinema Quarterly*, 1933.

[19] USA Today, "Picket Line, Not Catwalk, At 'Top Model'", 2006.

[20] William Booth, "Reality Is Only An Illusion, Writers Say", *Washington Post*, 2004.

[21] Spence, *Crafting Truth*, *p.* 11.

[22] Mary Gallagher, "ITV Extend Love Island Applications As They Search For 'Most Diverse Cast Ever' And Recruit 'All Shapes And Sizes'", *The Sun*, 2021.

[23] Robert J. Flaherty, *Nanook Of The North* (Inukjiak, 1922).

[24] Grierson, "The Documentary Producer", p. 8.

[25] Claude Massot, *Nanook Revisited* (Inukjiak, 1990).

[26] *Ibid.*

[27] Spence, *Crafting Truth*, p. 2.

References

Booth, William, "Reality Is Only An Illusion, Writers Say", Washington Post, 2004

Bruzzi, Stella, New Documentary: A Critical Introduction, 2nd ed. (Abingdon: Routledge, 2006)

Clissold, Bradley D., "Candid Camera And The Origins Of Reality TV", in Understanding Reality Television (London: Routledge, 2004)

Davis, Pete, "The John Quinoñes Panopticon", Current Affairs, 2022. <https://open.spotify.com/episode/1ibN7rfYEQVH X188HOCAwa?si=XVeNEFiERvi Ax6eRzYc4-A> [Accessed 6 February 2022]

Fenton, Andrew, "The Psychologist Behind Big Brother", News.Com.Au, 2012 <https://www.news.com.au/entertainment/tv/psychol ogist-behind-big-brother/newsstory/e193d00b9cc9a23be9917232d1a2e2 0c> [Accessed 6 February 2022]

Flaherty, Robert J., Nanook Of The North (Inukjiak, 1922).

Funt, Allen, and Philip Reed, Candidly, Allen Funt: A Million Smiles Later (New York: Barricade Books, 1994).

Gallagher, Mary, "ITV Extend Love Island Applications
    As They Search For 'Most Diverse Cast Ever' and
    Recruit 'All Shapes And Sizes'", The Sun, 2021

Grierson, John, "The Documentary Producer", Cinema
    Quarterly, 1933

Harrison, Ellie, "Here's How The Love Island Smoking
    Ban Will Work", Radio Times, 2018

Johnston, Elizabeth, "How Women Really Are: Disturbing
    Parallels between Reality Television and 18th Century
    Fiction", in How Real Is Reality TV?: Essays on
    Representation and Truth (North Carolina: McFarland,
    2006)

Massot, Claude, Nanook Revisited (Inukjiak, 1990)

McMullan, Thomas, "What Does The Panopticon Mean
    In The Age Of Digital Surveillance?", The Guardian,
    2015

Ophüls, Marcel, "Closely Watched Trains", in Claude
    Lanzmann's Shoah: Key Essays (New York: Oxford
    University Press Inc., 2007)

Orwell, George, 1984 (New York: Secker & Warburg,
    1949)

Sky News, "Love Island Stars To Be Offered Minimum Of
    Eight Therapy Sessions And Social Media Training
    After Show, ITV Says", 2021

Spence, Louise, and Vinicius Navarro, Crafting Truth:
    Documentary Form And Meaning (New Brunswick,
    N.J.: Rutgers University Press, 2011)

USA Today, "Picket Line, Not Catwalk, At 'Top Model'",
2006

Acknowledgements

To my Grandpa, whose wisdom in literature and life is vast, thank you for your advice on this book and your belief in my scholarly pursuits. To Jacquie Cameron, my disability advisor, I really couldn't have gotten through my time at university without you, thank you. To my parents, who gave me life, listen to every essay I have ever written, and sometimes understand what I am on about. To Tilda and Iona, for reading this dissertation in its draft stages, I appreciate you both. I would also like to thank my teachers throughout my undergraduate studies who made me a better writer, artist, and person; Kelly Egan, Rob Winger, Stephen Brown, John Bessai, Erica Eyres, Dr. Anna Notaro, Katie Potapoff, Josephine Jules Andrews, and Dr. Ana Salzberg. And finally, to my friends; I appreciate all of you that I can be my queer and rattling self around. You are the loves of my life.

56

Author Biography

Iona Rose Wheeler grew up near Glasgow and made films from a young age. After specialising in music during high school, Iona studied English and film studies at Dundee, and while on an exchange year in Ontario, Canada, they decided to pursue a degree in fine arts. They graduated from Duncan of Jordanstone College of Art and Design in 2022 with an experimental short film about lesbian intimacy and this dissertation, now a book, on reality television. Iona's queerness strongly influences their work, including their academic papers and poetry, which have been presented and published at institutions across Scotland, Europe, and Canada. You can find more at ionarw.com.

58

BOOM!

This book was originally submitted as a dissertation in partial fulfilment of the requirements of a Bachelor of Arts (Hons) degree in Fine Art at the Duncan of Jordanstone College of Art and Design, the University of Dundee, in 2022.

Iona Rose Wheeler

A note about Boom Graduates

We propel graduates forward so they can make their mark on the world - we push the boundaries, share brilliant ideas and inspire possibility. We publish dissertations as books, presented gift-boxed at graduation ceremonies, delivering brand-new research to the world quicker than anyone else. We plant trees for every commissioned book sold, and give our Boom graduates the chance to profit-share from their brilliant ideas. Furthermore we donate the majority of our profits to funding research and scholarship for disadvantaged students who wouldn't normally be able to attend university. Through academic excellence and environmental sustainability, Boom Graduates are changing the world.

We are Boom Graduates - an imprint of Boom Publications Ltd. We are a more-than-profit company, dedicating over half our profits to providing university scholarships for underprivileged students across the world. We aim to become the globe's biggest provider of such scholarships – and if like Iona, the author of this book, you'd also like to contribute to making the world a better place, please contact us: we publish monographs, edited books, and moreover our graduate series – Boom Graduates – are presented at graduation days across the world in archival, lined museum-quality presentation cases, engraved with the graduate's name and award.

Boom Publications are a spin out company from the Duncan of Jordanstone College of Art and Design, at the University of Dundee in Scotland. We were one of the winners of the 2022 Venture awards hosted by the Centre for Entrepreneurship, and finalists for the Converge Challenge, a national award that brings together ambitious and creative thinkers with innovative ideas to work with industry experts to transform their ideas into sustainable companies operating in the commercial world. We are also climate conscious and work with agencies to plant a tree for each and every book commissioned, offsetting thousands of tonnes of carbon each year. Follow us on social media to watch our forest grow @boomgraduates.

Thank you for contributing by purchasing this book. Please visit our catalogues at www.boompublications.com.

64

65

66

70

Iona Rose Wheeler

72

73

76

Iona Rose Wheeler

78

Reality Television & Representing Reality

79

81

82

83

Iona Rose Wheeler

84

Reality Television & Representing Reality

87

88